Captive
and Free

Insights from Galatians

Walter F. Taylor, Jr.

Augsburg Fortress, Minneapolis

Contents

INTERSECTIONS
Small Group Series

Captive and Free
Insights from Galatians

Developed in cooperation with the Division for Congregational Ministries

George W. Johnson, series introduction
David W. Anderson and Rich Gordon, editors
The Wells Group, series design
Dino Delano/AAA Stock Photos, cover photo

Scripture quotations are from New Revised Standard Version Bible, copyright 1989 Division of Christian
Education of the National Council of the Churches of Christ in the United States of America. Used by permission.

Introduction

Galatians: The charter of Christian freedom

Galatians is often called the charter of Christian freedom. In it the apostle Paul wrote such ringing and challenging statements as:

- ■ "Grace to you and peace from God our Father and the Lord Jesus Christ, who gave himself for our sins to set us free from the present evil age" (1:3-4a).

- ■ "But because of false believers secretly brought in, who slipped in to spy on the freedom we have in Christ Jesus, so that they might enslave us — we did not submit to them even for a moment" (2:4-5a).

- ■ "Christ redeemed us from the curse of the law by becoming a curse for us" (3:13a).

- ■ "For in Christ Jesus you are all children of God through faith" (3:26).

- ■ "For freedom Christ has set us free. Stand firm, therefore, and do not submit again to a yoke of slavery" (5:1).

- ■ "For you were called to freedom, brothers and sisters; only do not use your freedom as an opportunity for self-indulgence, but through love become slaves to one another" (5:13).

All of us feel bound in many ways. All of us want to feel free and, in fact, to be free in our daily lives, in our daily relationships, and in our daily walk with God.

Daily life

This study will help us identify the areas in our daily lives where we are enslaved, as well as those areas in which we are free. The study helps us to think through those areas using the Word of God as written in the New Testament letter to the Galatians. And this study helps us to experience the freedom God gives.

The study is designed so that the interaction between the Bible and your lives and relationships will lead to renewed appreciation of the relevance of Scripture for everyday living. In addition, the study provides the framework for growing insights into yourself and your relationships and skills in dealing with life's challenges.

But the study doesn't end there. It is also designed to turn you in an outward direction toward others in service.

God-self-others-Bible are the focus points of this course.

Main issues

The biblical text for our study is the book of Galatians. This letter was written by Paul to Christians who wanted to be free but who found slavery to old ways of living to be attractive. Among the topics to be discussed:

Theme 1
Christian freedom is a costly gift, gained through the life, death, and resurrection of Jesus Christ. His death frees us from sin, death, and fear. We trust God's action in Jesus to make us free. Thus we are freed by Jesus from fearing God so that we can love and worship God.

Theme 2
God frees us from guilt and self-salvation schemes, and restores our relationship with God. That is what we call justification, which is the opposite of trying to save ourselves by personal perfection. We identify with God's actions by our faith.

Theme 3
Christ gives us a new identity in Baptism— that of children of God. In God's new family, we are freed from evaluating people on the basis of race, status, and gender, and we become heirs of the promises of God.

Theme 4
People both inside and outside the church tempt us to relinquish our freedom. Paul exhorts us to resist every effort at subverting the good news.

Theme 5
The Spirit guides us to live in mutual support, concern, and love. The Spirit also works in us so that we arc freed to serve others through love. Trusting in God through Christ helps us to tap into a power that overcomes our inability to help others. That power is God's love.

Theme 6
Because of God's gifts to us, we are freed for others. Growth in service results in a renewed and profound sense of freedom for Christian living.

Small group process

Your small group is meant to be a laboratory for Christian thinking and living. It is a forum for sharing life experiences, for reflecting on the biblical texts and the issues for living that come from them, for giving and receiving feedback on interpretations and life concerns, and for providing and gaining from mutual support.

Each session makes connections with everyday life and draws implications for our relationships with family, friends, work associates, neighbors, and God.

Your small group is a setting in which people are able to share in an open, honest, and non-judgmental way. The group becomes also the home base for outreach and service to others.

SMALL GROUP SERIES

Welcome into the family of those who are part of small groups! Intersections Small Group Series will help you and other members of your group build relationships and discover ways to connect the Christian faith with your everyday life.

This book is prepared for those who want to make a difference in this world, who want to grow in their Christian faith, as well as for those who are beginning to explore the Christian faith. The information in this introduction to the Intersections small group experience can help your group make the most out of your time together.

Biblical encouragement

"Do not be conformed to this world, but be transformed by the renewing of your minds, so that you may discern what is the will of God—what is good and acceptable and perfect" (Romans 12:2).

Small groups provide an atmosphere where the Holy Spirit can transform lives. As you share your life stories and learn together, God's Spirit can work to enlighten and direct you.

Strength is provided to face the pressures to conform to forces and influences that are opposed to what is "good and acceptable and perfect." To "be transformed" is an ongoing experience of God's grace as we take up the cross and follow Jesus. Changed lives happen as we live in community with one another. Small groups encourage such change and growth.

What is a small group?

A number of definitions and descriptions of the small group ministry experience exist throughout the church. Roberta Hestenes, a Presbyterian pastor and author, defines a small group as an intentional face-to-face gathering of three to twelve people who meet regularly with the common purpose of discovering and growing in the possibilities of the abundant life.

Whatever definition you use, the following characteristics are important.

Small—Seven to ten people is ideal so that everyone can be heard and no one's voice is lost. More than 12 members makes genuine caring difficult.

Intentional—Commitment to the group is a high priority.

Personal—Sharing experiences and insights is more important than mastering content.

Conversational—Leaders that facilitate conversation, rather than teach, are the key to encouraging participation.

Friendly—Having a warm, accepting, non-judgmental atmosphere is essential.

Christ-centered—The small group experience is biblically based, related to the real world, and founded on Christ.

Features of Intersections Small Group Series

A small group model

A number of small group ministry models exist. Most models include three types of small groups:

- *Discipleship groups*—where people gather to grow in Christian faith and life;

- *Support and recovery group*s—which focus on special interests, concerns, or needs; and

- *Ministry groups*—which have a task-oriented focus.

Intersections Small Group Series presently offers material for discipleship groups and support and recovery groups.

For discipleship groups, this series offers a variety of courses with Bible study at the center. What makes a discipleship group different from traditional group Bible studies? In discipleship groups, members bring their life experience to the exploration of the biblical material.

For support and recovery groups, Intersections Small Group Series offers topical material to assist group members in dealing with issues related to their common experience, hurt, or interest. An extra section of facilitator helps in the back of the book will assist leaders of support and recovery groups to anticipate and prepare for special circumstances and needs that may arise as group members explore a topic.

Ministry groups can benefit from an environment that includes prayer, biblical reflection, and relationship building, in addition to their task focus.

Four essentials

Prayer, personal sharing, biblical reflection, and a group ministry task are part of each time you gather. These are all important for Christian community to be experienced. Each of the six chapter themes in each book includes:

- Short prayers to open and close your time together.

- Carefully worded questions to make personal sharing safe, non-threatening, and voluntary.

- A biblical base from which to understand and discover the power and grace of God. God's Word is the compass that keeps the group on course.

- A group ministry task to encourage both individuals and the group as a whole to find ways to put faith into action.

Flexibility

Each book contains six chapter themes that may be covered in six sessions or easily extended for groups that meet for a longer period of time. Each chapter theme is organized around two to three main topics with supplemental material to make it easily adaptable to your small group's needs. You need not use all the material. Most themes will work well for $1\frac{1}{2}$- to 2-hour sessions, but a variety of scheduling options is possible.

Bible based

Each of the six chapter themes in the book includes one or more Bible texts printed in its entirety from the New Revised Standard Version of the Bible. This makes it easy for all group members to read and learn from the same text. Participants will be encouraged through questions, with exercises, and by other group members to address biblical texts in the context of their own lives.

User friendly

The material is prepared in such a way that it is easy to follow, practical, and does not require a professional to lead it. Designating one to be the facilitator to guide the group is important, but there is no requirement for this person to be theologically trained or an expert in the course topic. Many times options are given so that no one will feel forced into any set way of responding.

Group goals and process

1. **Creating a group covenant or contract for your time together will be important.** During your first meeting, discuss these important characteristics of all small groups and decide how your group will handle them.

Confidentiality—Agreeing that sensitive issues that are shared remain in the group.

Regular attendance—Agreeing to make meetings a top priority.

Non-judgmental behavior—Agreeing to confess one's own shortcomings, if appropriate, not those of others, and not giving advice unless asked for it.

Prayer and support—Being sensitive to one another, listening, becoming a caring community.

Accountability—Being responsible to each other and open to change.

Items in your covenant should be agreed upon by all members. Add to the group covenant as you go along. Space to record key aspects is included in the back of this book. See page 60.

2. **Everyone is responsible for the success of the group, but do arrange to have one facilitator who can guide the group process each time you meet.**

The facilitator is not a teacher or healer. Teaching, learning, and healing happen from the group experience. The facilitator is more of a shepherd who leads the flock to where they can feed and drink and feel safe.

Remember, an important goal is to experience genuine love and community in a Christ-centered atmosphere. To help make this happen, the facilitator encourages active listening and honest sharing. This person allows the material to facilitate opportunities for self-awareness and interaction with others.

Leadership is shared in a healthy group, but the facilitator is the one designated to set the pace, keep the group focused, and enable the members to support and care for each other.

People need to sense trust and freedom as the group develops; therefore, avoid "shoulds" or "musts" in your group.

3. **Taking on a group ministry task can help members of your group balance personal growth with service to others.**

In your first session, identify ways your group can offer help to others within the congregation or in your surrounding community. Take time at each meeting to do or arrange for that ministry task. Many times it is in the doing that we discover what we believe or how God is working in our lives.

4. **Starting or continuing a personal action plan offers a way to address personal needs that you become aware of in your small group experience.**

For example, you might want to spend more time in conversation with a friend or spouse. Your action plan might state, "I plan to visit with Terry two times before our next small group meeting."

If you decide to pursue a personal action plan, consider sharing it with your small group. The group can be helpful in at least three ways: by giving support; helping to define the plan in realistic, measurable ways; and offering a source to whom you can be accountable.

5. **Prayer is part of small group fellowship.** There is great power in group prayer, but not everyone feels free to offer spontaneous prayer. That's okay.

Learning to pray aloud takes time and practice. If you feel uncomfortable, start with simple and short prayers. And remember to pray for other members between sessions.

Use page 61 in the back of this book to note prayer requests made by group members.

6. **Consider using a journal to help reflect on your experiences and insights between meeting times.**

Writing about feelings, ideas, and questions can be one way to express yourself; plus it helps you remember what so often gets lost with time.

The "Daily Walk" component includes material that can get your journaling started. This, of course, is up to you and need not be done on any regular schedule. Even doing it once a week can be time well spent.

How to use this book

The material provided for each session is organized around some key components. If you are the facilitator for your small group, be sure to read this section carefully.

The facilitator's role is to establish a hospitable atmosphere and set a tone that encourages participants to share, reflect, and listen to each other. Some important practical things can help make this happen.

- Whenever possible meet in homes. Be sure to provide clear directions about how to get there.

- Use name tags for several sessions.

- Place the chairs in a circle and close enough for everyone to hear and feel connected.

- Be sure everyone has access to a book; preparation will pay off.

Welcoming

The small group topic invites you to enter together into a journey of biblical and personal exploration. The main theme is freedom, so it is important that you have enough elbow room for the entire group. The meeting space needs to be large enough to allow you to meet as a whole group, as well as permitting you to break into groups of twos and threes.

Given the nature of the topic, it is important that people get to know and trust each other. The group also needs to give people latitude to say what they think and feel without fear of judgment.

Although the biblical texts are reproduced in the course book, the facilitator may want to have several Bibles available for reference.

Focus

Each of the six chapter themes in this book has a brief focus statement. Read it aloud. It will give everyone a sense of the direction for each session and provide some boundaries so that people will not feel lost or frustrated trying to cover everything. The focus also connects the theme to the course topic.

Community building

This opening activity is crucial to a relaxed, friendly atmosphere. It will prepare the ground for gradual group development. Two "Community Building" options are provided under each theme. With the facilitator giving his or her response to the questions first, others are free to follow.

One purpose for this section is to allow everyone to participate as he or she responds to non-threatening questions. The activity serves as a check-in time when participants are invited to share how things are going or what is new.

Make this time light and fun; remember, humor is a welcome gift. Use 15 to 20 minutes for this activity in your first few sessions and keep the entire group together.

During your first meeting, encourage group members to write down names and phone numbers (when appropriate) of the other members, so people can keep in touch. Use page 59 for this purpose.

Discovery

This component focuses on exploring the theme for your time together, using material that is read, and questions and exercises that encourage sharing of personal insights and experiences.

Reading material includes a Bible text with supplemental passages and commentary written by the topic writer. Have volunteers read the Bible texts aloud. Read the commentary aloud only when it seems helpful. The main passage to be used is printed so that everyone operates from a common translation and sees the text.

"A Further Look" is included in some places to give you additional study material if time permits. Use it to explore related passages and questions. Be sure to have your own Bible handy.

Questions and exercises related to the theme will invite personal sharing and storytelling. Keep in mind that as you listen to each other's stories, you are inspired to live more fully in the grace and will of God. Such exchanges make Christianity relevant and transformation more likely to happen. Caring relationships are key to clarifying one's beliefs. Sharing personal experiences and insights is what makes the small group spiritually satisfying.

Most people are open to sharing their life stories, especially if they're given permission to do so and they know someone will actively listen. Starting with the facilitator's response usually works best. On some occasions you may want to break the group into units of three or four persons to explore certain questions. When you reconvene, relate your experience to the whole group. The phrase "Explore and Relate," which appears occasionally in the margin, refers to this recommendation. Encourage couples to separate for this smaller group activity. Appoint someone to start the discussion.

Wrap-up

Plan your schedule so that there will be enough time for wrapping up. This time can include work on your group ministry task, review of key discoveries during your time together, identifying personal and prayer concerns, closing prayers, and the Lord's Prayer.

The facilitator can help the group identify and plan its ministry task. Introduce the idea and decide on your group ministry task during "Wrap-up" time in the first session. Tasks need not be grandiose. Activities might include:

- Ministry in your community, such as "adopting" a food shelf, clothes closet, or homeless shelter; sponsoring equipment, food, or clothing drives; or sending members to staff the shelter.

- Ministry to members of the congregation, such as writing notes to those who are ill or bereaved.

- Congregational tasks where volunteers are always needed, such as serving refreshments during the fellowship time after worship, stuffing envelopes for a church mailing, or taking responsibility for altar preparations for one month.

Depending upon the task, you can use part of each meeting time to carry out or plan the task.

In the "Wrap-up," allow time for people to share insights and encouragements and to voice special prayer requests. Just to mention someone who needs prayer is a form of prayer. The "Wrap-up" time may include a brief worship experience with candles, prayers, and singing. You might form a circle and hold hands. Silence can be effective. If you use the Lord's Prayer in your group, select the version that is known in your setting. There is space on page 62 to record the version your group uses. Another closing prayer is also printed on page 62. Before you go, ask members to pray for one another during the week. Remember also any special concerns or prayer requests.

Daily walk

Seven Bible readings and a thought, prayer, and verse for the journey related to the material just discussed are provided for those who want to keep the theme before them between sessions. These brief readings may be used for devotional time. Some group members may want to memorize selected passages. The Bible readings can also be used for supplemental study by the group if needed. Prayer for other group members can also be part of this time of personal reflection.

A word of encouragement

No material is ever complete or perfect for every situation or group. Creativity and imagination will be important gifts for the facilitator to bring to each theme. Keep in mind that it is in community that we are challenged to grow in Jesus Christ. Together we become what we could not become alone. It is God's plan that it be so.

For additional resources and ideas see *Starting Small Groups—and Keeping Them Going* (Minneapolis: Augsburg Fortress, 1995).

1 Christian Freedom: God's Gift

Jim Whitmer

Focus

Christian freedom is a costly gift, gained through the life, death, and resurrection of Jesus Christ. Christ's death frees us from sin, death, and fear.

For setting small group goals, see page 7.

List your goals and commitments in the appendix on page 60 for future reference.

Community building

- Look at the picture of a bird. What do you think of when you hear that someone "is free as a bird"? Share your reflections.

- This is a course on freedom—Christian freedom. It is also a study of a letter written by the early Christian missionary Paul. Discuss in the group what you would like to have happen in this course. Think about your goals. List them on page 60. Discuss them.

- Christian freedom includes service. The course is designed to have a service outreach project or ministry task. Think about ideas for this project. List and discuss them. The facilitator will help the group agree on its project.

- Discuss briefly the group covenant: meeting times, attendance, and confidentiality.

Option

We have heard about someone being "free as a bird." In your life, how free are you right now? Think of the animal and a short description of it that best describes how free you feel at this point in your life. Are you a caged lion, galloping horse, graceful gazelle, rat in a maze, finicky cat, lumbering ox, guard dog — or whatever?

In groups of three, share your animal and its description. In what ways do you see yourself as the animal you have chosen?

Opening prayer

Our loving God, we gather together today as people who sometimes feel free but who often feel much less than free. May your Spirit work in us so that we realize the freedom you give us in Christ. Amen.

Galatians 1:1-5

[1] "Paul an apostle—sent neither by human commission nor from human authorities, but through Jesus Christ and God the Father, who raised him from the dead—[2] and all the members of God's family who are with me,

To the churches of Galatia:

[3] Grace to you and peace from God our Father and the Lord Jesus Christ, [4] who gave himself for our sins to set us free from the present evil age, according to the will of our God and Father, [5] to whom be the glory forever and ever. Amen.

Is Jesus enough?

Our letter from Paul is addressed to Christians in Galatia, a region in central Turkey. Paul did not plan to do missionary work there, but a physical problem forced him to stop. He used the delay to tell people about Christ (Galatians 4:13-14). After he left, a troubling report reached him. He responded in 51-52 A.D. with the letter we are studying.

What Paul heard was that false teachers had come into the congregations. They told the recent converts that what Paul had said to them was not enough to help them. Paul had told the Galatians that all they had to do to be saved was to believe in Jesus as the Christ. The opponents said, "No, you must also be circumcised and become Jews." From the perspective of these Christians, a message without Jewish laws was incomplete.

For Paul the issue boiled down to: Is Jesus enough? Is it enough to believe in "Jesus only," or do we need to trust in "Jesus and . . . something else"? Can we trust Jesus alone to make us free?

Over against his opponents Paul began with the ringing claim: "Paul an apostle." What kind of apostle was he? "Sent neither by human commission nor from human authorities, but through Jesus Christ and God the Father" (1:1). An apostle is literally "one sent with a message." Paul asserted that his message came straight from God.

Paul, then, represented Jesus and the God "who raised him from the dead" (1:1). At the heart of his message was the death and resurrection of Jesus (Philippians 2:5-11). Jesus died willingly. He gave himself. Why? Paul gave two answers.

First, Jesus "gave himself for our sins" (Galatians 1:4). One of the most important words in Paul's vocabulary is the little word *for*. Jesus died for us, for our sins, in place of us. Paul's entire message can be summarized in this one preposition, *for*. So Christ frees us from sin.

Second, Jesus did this "to set us free from the present evil age." Jesus rescues us, delivers us from an existence that is alienated from God.

Discuss as a group.

- What, for Paul, was the basic "good news"?

- Christ "gave himself for." Discuss other examples of people giving themselves *for*.

- Has anyone ever given himself or herself for you? How did that make you feel?

- If you felt truly *free*, how would you live differently?

- What is sin? Please check the two definitions that most closely represent your thinking. Sin is:

  a. Not going to church on Sunday.
  b. Living as though God did not exist.
  c. Partying on Friday night.
  d. Cheating on income tax.
  e. Placing myself at the center of the world.
  f. Looking down on people who are different from me.

Choose two of the following. Share your responses in groups of two or three and give one or two reasons why you chose those responses.

Paul greeted the Galatians with a blessing: "Grace to you and peace . . ." (1:3). Grace means undeserved kindness and peace refers to God's gift of wholeness, health, contentment, and more through a loving relationship with God. Paul's greeting expresses the freeing power of a relationship to God through Jesus.

- What words or gestures do you receive that express divine grace and peace?

- What words or gestures do you extend to others to convey the freeing power of God's grace and peace?

- As a group, think of words and/or gestures you can use with each other that reflect the greeting to the Galatians.

A further look

Read Romans 5:6-8; 2 Corinthians 5:14-15,21; and 1 Thessalonians 5:9-11.

- According to Paul, what has Christ done for us?

- In your own words, tell one other person what Christ has done for you.

Galatians 3:13-14

¹³ Christ redeemed us from the curse of the law by becoming a curse for us—for it is written, "Cursed is everyone who hangs on a tree"—¹⁴in order that in Christ Jesus the blessing of Abraham might come to the Gentiles, so that we might receive the promise of the Spirit through faith.

The law of Moses—gift and curse

The law of Moses was originally a gracious gift of God (Romans 7:12). But when humanity misused that gift and sinned, the law condemned humanity and thus the law became a curse—in a way similar to the gift of sexuality and its misuse in our society. In the death of Jesus, God exhausted that curse. Jesus took the curse or judgment onto his shoulders and died for us.

If this first study is used for more than one small group session, introduce subsequent sessions with a "Community Builder" and "Prayer" and end with "Wrap-up."

In dying for our sins, Jesus also removed the outcome of sin, which is death. "For the wages of sin is death" (Romans 6:23). That removal does not mean that we will not physically die, but it does mean that it is not the end for those who trust in Jesus' death. That pact, in turn, means that death does not determine the meaning of our lives. Death, in fact, cannot separate us from the love of God in Jesus Christ (Romans 8:38-39). Therefore, we are freed from the fear of death.

The result of that freedom is the opposite of a curse—"the blessing of Abraham." In Genesis, God blessed Abraham by promising to be his God, to protect him, and to bless others through him (Genesis 12:1-3; 15:1-6). Paul saw that blessing extended to all believers, and so he said that all believers have God's Spirit in their lives. And as he wrote in 2 Corinthians 3:17, "where the Spirit of the Lord is, there is freedom." As we have seen, however, freedom from sin and death is a costly gift. It cost the life of Jesus.

Discuss as a group.

- Galatians 3:13 paints a gruesome picture. What does it tell you about how seriously God takes our sin?

- A well-known hymn begins, "In the cross of Christ I glory, Tow'ring o'er the wrecks of time." How are these lines helpful? How might they be dangerous?

- The second verse of the same hymn reads, "When the woes of life o'ertake me, Hopes deceive, and fears annoy, Never shall the cross forsake me; Lo, it glows with peace and joy." How do these lines comfort you and challenge you?

A further look

Read 1 Corinthians 1:18-25; Galatians 5:11; and Ephesians 2:15-16.

- What is the offense of the cross? Does the cross offend you? Should it?

- In what ways does the cross keep people away from Christianity? In what ways does it draw them in?

Discovery

Galatians 1:6-7,11-16

6 I am astonished that you are so quickly deserting the one who called you in the grace of Christ and are turning to a different gospel—7not that there is another gospel, but there are some who are confusing you and want to pervert the gospel of Christ.

11 For I want you to know, brothers and sisters, that the gospel that was proclaimed by me is not of human origin; 12for I did not receive it from a human source, nor was I taught it, but I received it through a revelation of Jesus Christ.

13 "You have heard, no doubt, of my earlier life in Judaism. I was violently persecuting the church of God and was trying to destroy it. 14I advanced in Judaism beyond many among my people of the same age, for I was far more zealous for the traditions of my ancestors. 15But when God, who had set me apart before I was born and called me through his grace, was pleased 16to reveal his Son to me, so that I might proclaim him among the Gentiles, I did not confer with any human being . . .

Paul is deserted

Galatians 1:6 is unique in Paul. In his other letters, immediately following the opening greetings (1:1-5) is a thanksgiving to God for the readers (see Romans 1:8-15). Here, Paul said he was amazed at these young-in-the-faith Christians. They had deserted him and turned to another gospel—except that there is no other gospel. In Greek, *gospel* means "good news." Paul used *gospel* as a shorthand term for the whole story of the wonderful good news of what God has done for us in Jesus. The opponents of Paul were trying to pervert that gospel by adding the law of Moses. For Paul that addition was a big mistake.

What was Paul's authority for saying this? He did not dream up this gospel, nor was it a human invention (Galatians 1:11-12). The source of this good news is the resurrected Jesus himself, who appeared to Paul on the road to Damascus (Acts 9:1-22).

The appearance of the Lord Jesus sharply changed Paul (Galatians 1:13-16). In his former life he sought to please God by observing the Commandments, even pleasing his superiors by persecuting Christians who claimed Jesus as the long-awaited Messiah (Christ). But as happens so often in the Bible, God broke in: "But when God" (see Ephesians 2:4). God set Paul apart, called him, and revealed Jesus to him (Galatians 1:15-16).

But that divine activity was not only for Paul's sake. God worked in Paul's life so that he, in turn, would proclaim Jesus among non-Jewish peoples (1:16). God broke through Paul's racial barrier (Paul himself was a Jew), so that the message of Jesus could go to all people.

Explore and relate. *Explore* in groups of three or four; then *relate* a brief summary to the entire group.

- For what life's work do you think you have been set apart? Explain.
- How can it make a difference to you to believe God is at work in your life on behalf of others?

Paul was able to overcome any fear he had in taking such a message to people who were different. He overcame his fears because he understood that no longer did he need to be afraid of God. We are freed by Jesus from fearing God to being able to love and worship God.

Discuss as a group.

- What other "gospels" compete in your world with the gospel of Jesus Christ? (Success, beauty, pleasure, winning?)
- What other "gospel" is for you most tempting?
- Paul reminded the Galatians of God's activity in his life. Share with another participant how God has worked in your life. In turn, listen to his or her story.
- If you cannot identify how God has worked in your life, share how you came to be in this group or how you came into the church. Perhaps your partner can help you find God's activity.

Consider this

Frederick Buechner says of the Bible: " . . . because it is a book about both the sublime and the unspeakable, it is a book also about life the way it really is. It is a book about people who at one and the same time can be both believing and unbelieving, innocent and guilty, crusaders and crooks, full of hope and full of despair. In other words it is a book about us.

"And it is also a book about God. If it is not about the God we believe in, then it is about the God we do not believe in. One way or another the story we find in the Bible is our own story."

From *Wishful Thinking: A Theological ABC* by Frederick Buechner
(New York: Harper and Row, 1973).

■ How is the Bible intended to be your story?

A further look

Read Acts 9:1-22; Mark 1:14-15; and Mark 5:21-24,35-43.

■ God moved Paul from persecutor to apostle. What barriers hinder you from moving more fully into the Christian faith? What does God need to help you overcome?

■ Jesus says to repent and believe in the good news. Of what do you need to repent?

■ What do you fear most? How has God freed you from those fears? What fears remain?

Wrap-up

See page 10 in the introduction for a description of "Wrap-up."

Before you go, take time for the following:

■ Group ministry task

■ Review

Ongoing prayer requests can be listed on page 61. See page 62 for suggested closing prayers.

■ Personal concerns and prayer concerns

■ Closing prayers

Daily walk

Bible readings

Day 1
Ephesians 2:11-13

Day 2
Ephesians 2:14-18

Day 3
Ephesians 2:19-22

Day 4
Philippians 2:5-11

Day 5
Romans 5:6-11

Day 6
Romans 6:17-23

Day 7
Romans 8:31-39

Thought for the journey

God's gifts to you today are grace, peace, and freedom. Look for those gifts: they are there. Relax, and thank God.

Prayer for the journey

Our gracious God, we thank you for the love you have shown us in the cross of Jesus. You have freed us. Help us to live in that freedom. Amen.

Verse for the journey

"Grace to you and peace from God our Father and the Lord Jesus Christ, who gave himself for our sins to set us free" (Galatians 1:3-4a).

2 Christian Freedom: Received by Faith

Focus

God frees us from self-salvation schemes, and restores our relationship with God. We identify with God's actions by our faith.

Community building

- Read each of the following quotations and state if you "agree," "disagree," or are "not sure":

  a. "To be free is to do your own thing."   —Pseudo-Plato

  b. "Freedom is not something that anybody can be given; freedom is something people take and people are as free as they want to be."
  From *Nobody Knows My Name* by James Baldwin (New York: Dial Press, 1961).

  c. "Freedom's just another word for nothin' left to lose, / Nothin' ain't worth nothin', but it's free."
  From "Me and Bobby McGee" by Kris Kristofferson and Fred Foster, 1969.

  d. "Oh, freedom! Oh, freedom! / Oh, freedom all over me! / When I am free! An' befo' I'd be a slave, / I'll buried in my grave, / An' go home to my Lord an' be free."

- Which statement most clearly expresses your concept of freedom? With which statement do you most strongly disagree?

Option

In groups of three, share your experiences from the past week.

When and where have you felt free? When and where have you felt un-free?

What people and situations seem to encourage you to be free? What people and situations seem to encourage you to feel "all tied up"?

Pray for each other. The prayers need only be one sentence long. Try to pick up on themes mentioned in the discussion.

Opening prayer

God, so much of our lives is spent in proving ourselves—to other people, to ourselves, even to you. Help us remember that in Jesus you have already approved us. Amen.

Galatians 2:16

16 We know that a person is justified not by the works of the law but through faith in Jesus Christ. And we have come to believe in Christ Jesus, so that we might be justified by faith in Christ, and not by doing the works of the law, because no one will be justified by the works of the law.

How have Christians been set free?

Christians, according to Paul, have been set free. But how are we set free? In 2:16 Paul stated the theme of his entire letter, and that thesis answers the question.

Negatively, we are not set free "by the works of the law." The laws of Moses do not free us, nor does any other attempt to earn our way to God by doing good things. God's law is a loving gift, but we turn it into a stepladder to God. We think that all God wants from us is outward, proper behavior, instead of an intimate relationship.

The result of trying to "make it on our own" is, ironically, captivity (see Ephesians 2:1-3). By trying to do what we do in every other area of our lives—earning our own way—we dig ourselves deeper into a bottomless hole. When will we have done enough so that God will love us? How can we ever be sure? The treadmill of trying to save ourselves by personal perfection never ends.

If true freedom cannot be earned, how can we "get" it? "A person is justified . . . through faith in Jesus Christ."

The words j*ustify* and *justification* come from the law court. Imagine that a prisoner stands before the judge. The prisoner is guilty. The moment for sentencing comes. But instead of condemning the prisoner to death or prison, the judge declares the guilty prisoner innocent and sets the prisoner free. The judge takes away the guilt, and so the prisoner is justified or "made right" by the judge.

The Greek word used by Paul for justification also means righteousness. In the Old Testament, to be righteous or just meant to uphold the relationship established by God in the covenant. When humanity breaks that relationship, we reject God and seek to replace God with other lords (Romans 1:18-32). But God remains true to the covenant with humanity and restores us to a positive relationship with God (Romans 3:21-26).

How does God do that? Through Christ. Why does God do that? "Out of the great love with which he loved us" (Ephesians 2:4; see also Romans 5:5,8). God makes us right with God through a free gift, a gift with which we identify by our faith.

Discuss as a group.

■ In your daily life, what do people mean when they say, "She is justifying herself"? How is that understanding of justification different from and similar to Paul's understanding?

■ During the last two weeks, in what ways have you justified yourself and your actions to:

Explore and relate.

    a. Your employer, supervisor, or customers
    b. Friends
    c. Parents
    d. Spouse
    e. Children
    f. God
    g. Yourself

■ What would it mean for the relationships listed above if you felt truly free from justifying yourself? Try to be as specific as possible.

A further look

Read Romans 1:18-25; Ephesians 2:1-3; and Romans 3:22b-24.

■ In what ways do you agree or disagree with the view that all of humanity has sinned?

■ Where in your life do you struggle most with sin?

■ Justification is a free gift. How do you receive gifts? Graciously? Warmly? With suspicion?

Galatians 2:19-20

[19] "For through the law I died to the law, so that I might live to God. I have been crucified with Christ; [20] and it is no longer I who live, but it is Christ who lives in me. And the life I now live in the flesh I live by faith in the Son of God, who loved me and gave himself for me."

Living to God

Remember, if this study theme is used for more than one small group session, introduce subsequent sessions with a "Community Builder" and "Opening Prayer" and end with "Wrap-up."

"To die to the law" means to have no further relationship to it as a means of making oneself right with God. The result is "living to God," being alive to God in a personal, dynamic way that is quite different from seeking to earn brownie points with God.

But that living to God also presumes death—*two* deaths. Christ has been crucified, but so have we. When we are baptized, we are identified with Jesus' death (Romans 6:4-8). Language of death reminds us of the sharp break and new directions in life that come when we believe in Jesus. This language also points in another direction: freedom from being so concerned about ourselves. We have died! What else is there to fear?

Not only have we died, but now Christ lives in us. When we live on our own, the only power for living we discover within us is our own power. But when we entrust our lives to God through Jesus, we find a new power in our lives, a new source of dynamic and purpose: Jesus.

This means that, for Paul, real freedom is not unbridled power to direct our own lives. Real freedom and life come as gifts from God. And who is this God? This is the God who sent the Son, "who loved me and gave himself for me." Jesus died for the whole world: yes! But Jesus also died for each of us individually, for you and for me.

Discuss as a group.

■ The bad news is, "You have died." The good news is, "You have died." How do you make sense of these statements?

■ Pair up with another person and discuss:

    a. To what parts of your past and present would you like to die?

    b. What is keeping you from doing that?

■ Think of people who don't care what others think of them. What is positive about that attitude? What is negative? Do you care what others think about you? In what ways does that concern limit you?

■ "It is no longer I who live, but it is Christ who lives in me" (2:20). What is there about this statement that is of particular importance to you at this time in your life?

Choose one and explain.

a. I am freed from selfish desires and freed for others.
b. God is at work in my life, including my desires and actions.
c. My value as a person is based on what God has done for me through Christ; it is not based on my efforts.
d. I am captive to the love of God.
e. I am freed from the negative judgments of others.
f. I am freed from my own self-condemning judgments.
g. This statement makes life easier.
h. This statement makes life more difficult.
i. Other.

Respond as a group.

Consider this

I know two men. One of them works fourteen hours a day, seven days a week, at least 360 days a year. His pay is modest. He is a baker whose life is sharply controlled by his work. The other man is a highly-educated professional who travels to exotic destinations, dines at fancy restaurants, and drives the latest cars.

Who is free? Who is enslaved? The baker literally "whistles while he works." He loves his family and enjoys every minute with them. While he works hard, he trusts in God for his daily well-being. The professional trusts in his education and his abilities. God is at best an afterthought. In his third marriage, this wealthy, "successful" man struggles to control alcohol and other drug habits. Who is free and who is enslaved?

A further look

Read Romans 6:3-4; Romans 6:5-8; and Romans 7:6.

■ In Christianity freedom comes through death. How do you see that happening in the life of Jesus? In your own life?

■ Discuss with two other people your responses to the question, "What does baptism mean to you?"

Galatians 3:2-7

2 **The only thing I want to learn from you is this: Did you receive the Spirit by doing the works of the law or by believing what you heard?** 3**Are you so foolish? Having started with the Spirit, are you now ending with the flesh?** 4**Did you experience so much for nothing?—if it really was for nothing.** 5**Well then, does God supply you with the Spirit and work miracles among you by your doing the works of the law, or by your believing what you heard?**

6 **Just as Abraham "believed God, and it was reckoned to him as righteousness,"** 7**so, you see, those who believe are the descendants of Abraham.**

Faith: A looking, listening, and believing trust

Paul's opponents believed that salvation depended on doing the works outlined by Moses' law. Paul countered with two arguments.

The first argument is from experience. Paul asked, "How do we identify with what God is doing for us?" His example is the reception of the Holy Spirit. Was it by doing works that his readers received that gift, or was it by believing what they heard?

If the answer is "by doing works," we are back to the unending treadmill of justifying ourselves.

When we believe, on the other hand, we rely not on ourselves but on what we have heard. And what we have heard is a message about what God has done for us.

Paul's second argument is the example of Abraham. In Genesis, God had promised to make of Abraham and Sarah a great nation. But so far the couple was childless. In 15:1-5, God directed Abraham to gaze at the sky. Once more, God promised him descendants—as many as the stars. And what did Abraham do, as he tried to count the stars, as he counted the number of children he and Sarah had—none? "He believed the LORD; and the LORD reckoned it to him as righteousness" (15:6).

What is faith, according to Paul? Faith is a looking, a listening, and a believing trust.

■ The facilitator will provide blindfolds. Form pairs. One member of each pair is blindfolded. The other is the guide. For five minutes the guides take their partners on a tour of the meeting space or adjacent area. Guides speak as little as possible and guide by touch; guides probably will want to hold the hand or arm of their partner. At the end of the walk, switch roles.

Discuss as a group.

a. What was it like not to see?
b. What was it like being the guide?
c. What signals did the blindfolded find helpful?
d. When you were blindfolded, did you trust your guide? All the time? If not, when did you feel a lack of trust? What helped you trust your guide?
e. What is difficult about trusting?

■ Faith is sometimes viewed like a train station or an airport. It is a goal. When it is reached, everything should be fine. Others see faith as a journey, but one with no step-by-step directions or maps. Which view is closer to your understanding?

Explore and relate.

■ Where is your life of faith these days? Where are you headed? What major landmarks have you passed in the last week? year? five years?

Respond as a group.

Consider this

Because of an accident while horseback riding, I am tentative about riding. A recent vacation in Colorado put me to the test. We rented horses for an hour's ride. Within five minutes the guide was leading us down hills, up hills, over rocky areas, along extremely narrow paths, through mud, and often with a sharp drop-off to the side. My horse "Lobo" and I quickly came to an understanding: he knew the way and he didn't want to fall any more than I did. Once I trusted him to do his job, I relaxed and enjoyed a memorable ride along the western Rockies.

■ **How is this story like or unlike the Christian faith?**

A further look

Read Genesis 15:1-6; John 1:35-42; and Romans 10:13-15.

■ In what ways is it important for you to hear the story of what God has done?

■ How important for you is telling the story?

■ Share with another person the first time you were told God's story.

Wrap-up

See page 10 in the introduction for a description of "Wrap-up."

Before you go, take time for the following:

- Group ministry task

- Review

- Personal concerns and prayer concerns

- Closing prayers

Ongoing prayer requests can be listed on page 61. See page 62 for suggested closing prayers.

Daily walk

Bible readings

Day 1
Mark 9:16-27

Day 2
John 4:39-42

Day 3
John 4:46-54

Day 4
Romans 1:16-17

Day 5
Romans 3:19-22a

Day 6
Romans 4:18-25

Day 7
Romans 10:8-13

Thought for the journey

Today God frees you from the need to justify yourself. Trust God's gift and live in it.

Prayer for the journey

We praise you, O Lord, because you make us right with you apart from any good things we can do. It all depends on you. Help us to believe that. Amen.

Verse for the journey

"We have come to believe in Christ Jesus, so that we might be justified by faith in Christ" (Galatians 2:16).

3 Christian Freedom: A New Identity

Focus

Christ gives us a new identity: children of God. In God's new family, we are freed from evaluating people on the basis of race, status, and gender.

Discovery

- You have been together as a group for a while now and know a fair amount about each other. Share in the whole group the three identities you have that most clearly define who you are: for example, Christian, mother, tax preparer. Then tell the other participants how these identities free you, bind you, or do both. In particular, focus on your activities of the last two weeks.

- After all have had a chance to share, pray for each other. The facilitator starts by praying for the person on his or her right. That person prays for the individual to her or his right, and so on. The prayers need be only a sentence or two long. In them, celebrate the freedoms people experience in their identities and ask for God's power and strength where people feel bound.

Option

Item: One in five U.S. children under the age of 18 is poor (13.4 million children). Children are twice as likely to be poor than the elderly.

Item: In 1991, 35.7 million Americans were listed as poor. That is 14.2 percent of the population.

In groups of three, reflect on where in your world people are denied freedom because of their identities—racial, gender, religious, economic, social, or others. Pray about those situations. What can you do to increase their (and your) opportunities for freedom?

Opening prayer

Our Creator, you have made us, and you have given us many identities. We praise you for adopting us as your children through the waters of baptism. In the name of Jesus, your son, we pray. Amen.

Galatians 3:26-27

26 In Christ Jesus you are all children of God through faith. 27 As many of you as were baptized into Christ have clothed yourselves with Christ.

The children of God

In 3:26 Paul wrote to "you," referring to the Gentile Christians of Galatia (central Turkey). And what about the "you" in 3:27? They are the children of God. Paul, of course, was a Jewish Christian. In the Old Testament and in the Jewish tradition, only Jews were considered to be the children of God (Deuteronomy 14:1, for example). Paul extended that title of honor to Gentiles.

From the traditional perspective of Paul's people, that extension was scandalous enough. But how is that title extended to non-Jews? Not on the basis of conversion to Judaism but by faith in Jesus as the Christ. Paul thereby gave Christians a new identity by defining our status before God: we are not foreigners to God, we are God's own children (Galatians 4:4-7).

In 3:27-28, Paul used language from an early baptismal service. Everyone who has been baptized into Christ has new clothes! The new clothes don't consist of a dress or a suit. The new clothes are Christ himself. Putting on certain clothing is often a sign of status. Aaron and his sons wore special clothing when serving as priests (Exodus 28:40-43), and the restoration to the status of son became complete when the prodigal was given the best robe (Luke 15:22). What clothing could be more important than Christ? And who is he? He is the Son, the Child of God. And so the Christian is "covered" by the Son and is made by him into a child of God.

Baptism radically changes who we are. It gives us a new identity as God's children. Further, "clothed yourselves with Christ" means that the baptized take on Christ's characteristics. There is a family resemblance! Perhaps that is why early Christians called each other sister and brother.

Discuss as a group.

- How do you "resemble" other members of the Christian family? How do you not resemble them?

- What are the two most important aspects of your Christian identity? How do these parts of who you are help you in your relationships with others?

- You are a child of God. How does that affect your understanding of who you are in your immediate family, in your extended family, at work, in the neighborhood, and in the church?

- How does the image of being clothed with Christ free you? How does it make you captive?

A further look

Read Romans 13:12-14; Ephesians 6:11-17; and Colossians 3:12-15.

- We put on our clothes every day. What difference would it make in your daily relationships if each morning you thought of putting on the Lord Jesus?

- Where in your life would wearing the armor of God be helpful?

- What two virtues or characteristics listed in our passages would be most helpful to you in the coming week? Pray for these gifts.

Discovery

Galatians 3:28

28 There is no longer Jew or Greek, there is no longer slave or free, there is no longer male and female; for all of you are one in Christ Jesus.

"There is no longer ..."

The results of being clothed with Christ, of being children of God, are outlined in this verse. First Paul stated the results negatively: "There is no longer." Paul took up the three major divisions of his day that, on the one hand, separated people, and yet on the other hand provided the foundation for society:

"There is no longer Jew or Greek." From the Jewish side, the distinction was Jew-Gentile; from the Greek side it was Greek-barbarian, but in either case the racial and cultural division was basic.

"There is no longer slave or free." The slave-free distinction was dramatic and had the most profound social and economic implications.

"There is no longer male and female." Women were generally placed into a secondary role.

For Paul, God frees us from evaluating people on the basis of race, status, and gender. While in this world the distinctions continue to exist, value judgments and behaviors based on them are not to be part of the life of the church. And so Paul founded congregations that upheld the equality of women and men, that freely admitted both slave and free, and that included people of different ethnic origins.

Paul also stated in a positive way the results of being clothed with Christ: "all of you are one in Christ Jesus." Just as Christ is not to be divided, so the believers themselves are not to be separated from each other (1 Corinthians 1:10-17). We are united. Our unity transcends our limitations as well as the value judgments we tend to place on our natural distinctions.

How does all of this happen? "In Christ Jesus." Through our baptisms into Christ, God has given us a new identity that unites us with other believers.

Explore and relate.

■ When I see someone for the first time, I usually evaluate the person on the basis of (check all that apply):

a. Looks	f. Gender
b. Clothes	g. Language
c. Age	h. Occupation, if known
d. Skin color	i. Pattern of speech
e. Hairstyle	j. Other

■ How reliable do you find these criteria? In what ways do they help you get to know a person? In what ways do they create barriers?

Discuss as a group.

■ What do you see as the major divisions between people today? Use those divisions and update Paul's statement in 3:28. For example, "There are no longer Dodger and Giant fans."

■ In your daily living, what differences between people make it especially hard for you to relate to another person (age, education, gender, color, and so on)? Think of a time when you have been able to overcome those differences. What made that possible? What does God have to do with the overcoming of such differences?

A further look

Read 1 Corinthians 12:12-13; Galatians 6:15; and 2 Corinthians 5:16-17.

- Count the number of times the word *one* appears in 1 Corinthians 12:12-13. What does it mean to you to say, "Christians are one"?

- What does it mean to regard people "from a human point of view"? What difference would it make to see people as God's "new creations"?

Discovery

Galatians 3:29—4:1,4-7

29 **And if you belong to Christ, then you are Abraham's offspring, heirs according to the promise.** 4:1 **My point is this: heirs, as long as they are minors, are no better than slaves, though they are the owners of all the property; . . .** 4**But when the fullness of time had come, God sent his Son, born of a woman, born under the law,** 5**in order to redeem those who were under the law, so that we might receive adoption as children.** 6**And because you are children, God has sent the Spirit of his Son into our hearts, crying, "Abba! Father!"** 7**So you are no longer a slave but a child, and if a child then also an heir, through God.**

The children of Abraham

Verse 29 concludes Galatians 3 and returns us to Abraham. In 3:6-7 Paul raised the issue of who are Abraham's real children. In 3:29 he completed his answer: the ones belonging to Christ are Abraham's children. Why? We belong to Christ through faith. And who is Abraham? The one who believed (3:6). And so "those who believe are the descendants of Abraham" (3:7).

Paul went a step further. If we are descendants, then we are also heirs. But being heirs is no advantage if we are minors and unable to inherit. Nothing belongs to us as long as we are underage (4:1). We might as well be slaves.

Galatians 4:4-6 outlines God's response. God sent his Son Jesus to redeem. To redeem something is to buy it back. The term was especially used for the buying back—and release—of a slave. Jesus came to buy us back from everything that enslaves, and he came to set us free (3:13). The term has strong

Old Testament connections, since the God of Israel is the God who redeems the people from slavery in Egypt (Deuteronomy 21:8; 24:18).

The purpose of the redeeming activity of Jesus is "that we might receive adoption as children." We are God's adult children, whom God has given an astounding gift, the Spirit. And that Spirit enables us to cry out, "Abba! Father!" The word *abba* is Aramaic. It indicates an intimate relationship between parent and child and is the same term used by Jesus in addressing God.

How do children greet their father? They say, "Daddy." Our adoption as God's children gives us the right to address God as loving father, as loving parent.

That is not a natural right but a gift from God. The final outcome is that we are no longer slaves. We are God's children and inheritors of the promises of God (Galatians 4:7).

Discuss as a group.

■ "Father Abraham had many kids, many kids had Father Abraham," so goes the song. Who are Abraham's children?

■ What should they do about those who are not Abraham's children?

■ We are adopted children. How might that affect our attitude toward those who are not yet adopted?

■ You are God's heir. What inheritance do you have from God right now?

Mark all that apply.

    a. Assurance of God's love.
    b. Material security.
    c. Eternal life.
    d. Daily living without stress.
    e. Close relationships with people.
    f. A throne in heaven.
    g. Eternal life.
    h. Happiness.
    i. Financial success.
    j. Triumph over my enemies.

■ What inheritance do you expect from God in the future? Use the same list again.

■ Discuss your choices with two other people. What other "inheritances" do you want to list?

■ Children show their parents' characteristics (just as the children of faithful Abraham have faith). Who are your parents or big sisters or brothers in the faith? How do you reflect their characteristics? Who is your child in the faith?

Consider this

In the 1930s my grandparents had two dear friends named Billie and Paul. After years of trying unsuccessfully to conceive their own biological child, Billie and Paul decided to adopt. My grandparents went with them to the hospital. Before they went into the nursery, the nurse told Billie and Paul, "Take your time. Look around until you find the baby you want." Paul exploded. "You don't go shopping for a baby! The very first child we see, that child will be ours." . . . And who are we? God's adopted children.

A further look

Read Romans 8:14-17; Mark 14:32-36; and Ephesians 1:3-6.

■ Think of a time when a parent was angry with you. What emotions did you feel? What do you feel when Paul says that being children of God means adoption, not fear?

■ Share stories about adoption: your own, your children's, others known to you. What special gifts are given in adoption?

Wrap-up

Before you go, take time for the following:

- Group ministry task

- Review

- Personal concerns and prayer concerns

- Closing prayers

Daily walk

Bible readings

Day 1
Colossians 3:9-11

Day 2
John 1:10-13

Day 3
1 John 3:1-2

Day 4
John 17:20-23

Day 5
2 Corinthians 1:18-20a

Day 6
Hebrews 9:13-15

Day 7
Hebrews 11:8-12

Thought for the journey

You are a child of God! God loves you. And God loves each person you will deal with today. Seek to live in that love.

Prayer for the journey

We thank you, O God, for making us who we are: your beloved children. Free us to share your love with at least one other person today. Amen.

Verse for the journey

"In Christ Jesus you are all children of God through faith" (Galatians 3:26).

4 Christian Freedom: Always Threatened

People both inside and outside the church tempt us to relinquish our freedom. Paul exhorts us to resist every effort that subverts the good news.

Community building

"Englishmen never will be slaves: they are free to do whatever the Government and public opinion allow them to do."
—George Bernard Shaw

Split into two groups to discuss these questions.

- How free do you feel today?

- In what areas of your life do you feel most free? Least free? What makes the difference?

- Think of a time in your life when you became free of a bad habit but then returned to it. Why did you make that decision or have that relapse? What made it hard for you to stay free of that habit?

- What factors in your life make it difficult to live in freedom?

Option

Using the first letter of your first name, think of one adjective that begins with that letter and that describes your mood today (example: Winnie describes herself as wild, wonderful, or weary). If you are stumped, use the first letter of your last name.

Share your adjective and the current life situations that led you to choose that adjective. Respond with sentence prayers for each other.

Opening prayer

You have given us so much, O Lord, including the gift of freedom. Keep us from denying that freedom and embracing sin. We pray in the name of Jesus, whose cross makes us free. Amen.

Galatians 2:1,3-5

¹ Then after fourteen years I went up again to Jerusalem with Barnabas, taking Titus along with me. . . . ³ But even Titus, who was with me, was not compelled to be circumcised, though he was a Greek. ⁴ But because of false believers secretly brought in, who slipped in to spy on the freedom we have in Christ Jesus, so that they might enslave us—⁵ we did not submit to them even for a moment, so that the truth of the gospel might always remain with you.

The debate over circumcision

Fourteen years after his first visit to Jerusalem as a Christian, Paul went again to the city. The meeting he attended was called the Apostolic Council and was held to clarify how the young church could carry out evangelism among non-Jews as well as Jews.

Paul knew that not all Christians agreed with his understanding of a Christian faith free of the Jewish law. Some Christians (the "false believers" in 2:4) believed that non-Jews had first to be circumcised—and thus become Jews—before they could become Christians.

Barnabas and Titus went with Paul. Titus was a Gentile convert who had never been circumcised. He became for this meeting the primary test case: would the Jerusalem apostles demand that he be circumcised? They did not, and so Paul's gospel was reaffirmed (2:3).

The so-called false believers did not agree. For them, Paul was giving away the company store for nothing in return! He was too free with the good news. Unless people were first bound by the law, they could not become Christians.

For Paul the truth of the gospel was at stake (2:5), and so he did not yield. The Jerusalem apostles, in turn, approved his work (2:6-9).

■ In what ways might Christian freedom be frightening to you?

Choose your two strongest responses and explain.

    a. I need clear guidelines.
    b. I don't trust myself to be free.
    c. Sin is too strong in me.
    d. I have seen people misuse freedom.
    e. Other concerns.

Paul took a strong stand against false belief. Most of us live lives that are less public than Paul's. Keeping our faith is less a matter of making dramatic public statements and more a matter of not allowing our faith to be chipped away.

- What chips away at your faith?

- What are the regular events or thoughts that make it hard for you to believe?

- What makes it difficult to have strong convictions? What resources in the Christian faith make it easier?

Consider this

Early in our marriage, my wife and I corresponded with our families by exchanging audio tapes. When my sister-in-law was in high school, she told us that she had been invited to a party that "everybody" was going to attend. She had neglected to tell her parents that the party was at a cabin, and no adults would be present. She wasn't sure she should attend. Her parents had refused to say yes or no. They had given her the freedom to decide for herself. What she told us was that she wished her parents would simply say no, so she wouldn't have to make the decision. She found freedom frightening.

- Read the story above and share examples of when you or others shied away from freedom.

A further look

Read Galatians 2:6-10; Acts 15:22-29; and 2 Corinthians 8:1-5.

- In Galatians 2, Paul outlined his specific mission field and that of the Jerusalem apostles. What is your specific mission field? Where can you—and perhaps only you—be a witness for Christ?

- In 2 Corinthians 8, Paul wrote about the collection for the Christian poor mentioned in Galatians 2:10. Sometimes a project that helps other people can aid us in overcoming our differences. Share examples. How is your service outreach project or ministry task going? How has it affected relationships within your group?

Galatians 2:11-12,14

11 But when Cephas came to Antioch, I opposed him to his face, because he stood self-condemned; 12for until certain people came from James, he used to eat with the Gentiles. But after they came, he drew back and kept himself separate for fear of the circumcision faction. . . . 14But when I saw that they were not acting consistently with the truth of the gospel, I said to Cephas before them all, "If you, though a Jew, live like a Gentile and not like a Jew, how can you compel the Gentiles to live like Jews?"

Eating with Gentiles

Most of us don't eat with just anybody. We are selective. So was Cephas (Peter). He had been eating with Gentile Christians. That meant that not only was he eating regular meals with Gentiles, but he was also sharing the Lord's Supper with them. The Lord's Supper was eaten within the context of a larger meal—a potluck, in fact!

Jewish people who wanted to be ritually pure could not eat with Gentiles, but Paul's gospel said that value judgments based on the Jew-Gentile distinction no longer counted (Galatians 3:28). And so Jewish Christians like Peter and Paul were free to eat with Gentile Christians.

Or at least Peter felt free until people came from Jerusalem to Antioch, in Syria. When they raised questions, Peter stopped eating with Gentiles. He separated himself from them, refusing even to have communion with non-Jewish believers.

Paul, who thought things had been worked out at Jerusalem, confronted Peter. He charged Peter with living inconsistently with the truth of the gospel.

Peter had lost his vision of what God was doing. He could look only to past ways of doing things.

In Galatians 2 we see that the temptation to give up Christian freedom came from other Christians as well as from within Peter himself. Peter lost the center of freedom in Christ, and he stood, said Paul, self-condemned (2:11).

Imagine you are Peter. Why might you have problems with Paul's message of salvation apart from Jewish law? Rank the following reasons from 1 to 5, with 1 being the most important reason.

__ Paul has gone too far with this freedom stuff.
__ We really should return to the traditions of the past.
__ God doesn't want the chosen people to mix with outsiders.
__ We need to be careful; we don't want to move too fast for people.
__ We've never done it this way before.

Share your rankings and thinking.

What is attractive about Peter's position?

Another reason for Peter's wavering may have been his desire not to appear different from other Jewish people. The security of old patterns beckoned him. How does that fit or not fit with the following quotation?

"The man who hangs on the cross has surrendered every kind of human security, and those who follow him must surrender it too." From *Freedom and Obligation* by C.K. Barrett (Philadelphia: Westminster Press, 1985).

What does this quotation say to you?

Ernst Kurtz and Katherine Ketcham wrote, "*So long as we cling, we are bound. . . .* Yet the alcoholic—and the rest of us, in one way or another—hang on." (From *The Spirituality of Imperfection.* New York: Bantam Books, 1964.) To what are you clinging? How does it bind you and keep you from freedom?

Write a table grace that gives thanks for food and freedom in Christ.

A further look

Read Matthew 9:9-13; 1 Corinthians 11:17-26; and John 8:31-36.

With whom do you eat?

In what ways can eating with certain people open doors or create barriers?

How in the last week has the truth freed you from what you want to cling to?

Galatians 5:1

¹ For freedom Christ has set us free. Stand firm, therefore, and do not submit again to a yoke of slavery.

Christ frees us

Galatians 5:1a is one of the New Testament's most beautifully compact statements of the good news. Christ is the subject, not human achievement. Christ frees. And Christ frees us.

In light of their freedom, Paul exhorted the Galatians: "Do not submit again to a yoke of slavery." Paul referred to a special yoke that was hung around the neck of a slave whose spirit the master wanted to break. By that image Paul warned the Galatians that freedom can be lost.

But why did Christ free us? "For freedom." That is, the destiny of the Christian is freedom, and the purpose of Christ's activity is to give freedom. The goal of Christian life, said Paul, as well as its foundation, is freedom.

The language Paul used here likely came from a ceremony in which a slave who had saved enough money went to a temple and paid the purchase price to the priests. They in turn bought the slave in the name of their god. The former slave now was legally free. The slave was purchased, say ancient records, "for freedom," that is, in order to be free. The former slave obviously would avoid returning to the former status of slave. And so Paul warned his readers to avoid falling back into their previous condition as slaves of sin.

The positive directive that Paul gave was: "Stand firm." Stand firm against everything that tries to push you down.

Discuss as a group.

- Read these lines: "COME TO THE EDGE." / "No, we will fall." / "COME TO THE EDGE." / "No, we will fall." / They came to the edge. / He pushed them, and they flew."
  —Guillaume Apollinaire

- Do you remember the picture on page 11 of the bird, and the line, "Free as a bird"? What forces outside you and inside you are keeping you from "flying" in freedom?

■ Think about an aspect or area of your life where you feel God may be leading you to new levels of freedom. Where, for example, is growth taking place for you in your relationships with other people and with God? Where do you especially feel the need for further growth?

■ To what slaveries from your past do you now refuse to submit?

■ Paul defended a faith freed from legalistic restraints. How are you tempted to live by the "letter of the law" as a way to avoid the freedom of loving choices?

Choose one and explain.

a. Pay taxes without regard for how those taxes are used.
b. Accept public opinion without objecting to how it might treat others unfairly.
c. Stay out of trouble but do not take initiative to help someone in need.
d. Avoid resolving conflicts because you think to yourself that the problem was not your fault.
e. Avoid contact with another generation—or any other group—because they are "different."
f. Other.

■ How are you tempted to be "slaves of sin"?

Choose one and explain.

a. Overconcern with personal image.
b. Need for control in relationships.
c. "Having a good time" becomes more valuable than nurturing caring and responsible relationships.
d. A slave of demanding schedules that take you away from valued relationships or commitments.
e. Personal interests become more important than time for prayer and praise to God.
f. Other.

A further look

Read 1 Corinthians 16:13-14; Philippians 3:17—4:1; and Philippians 1:27-29.

■ During the coming days, in what two ways do you want to "stand firm" in your Christian freedom?

■ What does it mean to you to live "life in a manner worthy of the gospel of Christ"?

■ How is suffering for Christ a privilege?

Wrap-up

Before you go, take time for the following:

- Group ministry task

- Review

- Personal concerns and prayer concerns

- Closing prayers

Daily walk

Bible readings

Day 1
Romans 8:1-2

Day 2
Galatians 4:21-26

Day 3
Isaiah 58:6-9a

Day 4
Isaiah 61:1-4

Day 5
Revelation 5:6-10

Day 6
Titus 2:11-14

Day 7
1 Peter 1:18-21

Thought for the journey

"The freedom which is given in Christ is radical insecurity from the human standpoint. . . . For our only security is Christ."

From *The Ethics of Freedom* by Jacques Ellul. (Grand Rapids, MI: William B. Eerdmans Publishing Co., 1976.)

Prayer for the journey

Help us this day, O Lord, to stand firm. Events and people push us here, pull us there. Help us to remember the center of our lives, Christ. Amen.

Verse for the journey

"For freedom Christ has set us free. Stand firm, therefore, and do not submit again to a yoke of slavery" (Galatians 5:1).

5 Christian Freedom: Guided by the Spirit

Focus

The Spirit guides us to live in mutual support, concern, and love. The Spirit also works in us so that we are freed to serve others through love.

Community building

- Begin with silence. After a few moments, pray: "Give us, O Lord, the ability to focus, the ability to center ourselves in you during this time. We pray that you would give that gift to . . . [name each member of the group], and to me. In Jesus' name. Amen." Silence follows.

- Read aloud Galatians 5:24: "And those who belong to Christ Jesus have crucified the flesh with its desires and passions." Reflect privately about that verse: How have you crucified your flesh? Where do you need yet to crucify your flesh?

- Read aloud Galatians 5:25: "If we live by the Spirit, let us also be guided by the Spirit." Reflect silently about that verse: How do you live by the Spirit?

- Share a time when you believe you were guided by the Spirit of God.

Option

Capital University President Josiah Blackmore called David Warren, former president of Ohio Wesleyan University, to ask Dr. Warren if he believed in free speech. "Of course I do," he responded. "All college presidents believe in free speech." "Good," said Dr. Blackmore. "How would you like to give one?" And so Warren agreed to speak to the Columbus Rotary Club—for no charge.

Dr. Warren found that belief in freedom leads to responsibility. What responsibilities go with Christian freedom?

Opening prayer

Help us, O God, to be open to the presence and guidance of your Holy Spirit as we meet today. May your Spirit lead us into new paths of service. In Jesus' name. Amen.

Galatians 5:6-7

6 For in Christ Jesus neither circumcision nor uncircumcision counts for anything; the only thing that counts is faith working through love. 7 You were running well; who prevented you from obeying the truth?

Faith is energized through love

Galatians 5:6 reminds us of the discussion regarding Jew and Gentile and whether a Gentile had first to become a Jew before becoming a Christian. Those distinctions no longer count. What counts is a faith that works through love.

We tend to think of our faith only in relationship to God (Galatians 3–4). But faith is not only a matter of the believer's relationship with God, for God transforms the believer as that relationship develops. Faith-filled people cannot be closed to the human needs around them.

And so faith works, it labors. Does that mean that we are back at the point where we are trying to save ourselves by our good deeds? Not at all. The good deeds, in fact, are a natural result of faith. Trusting in God through Christ helps us to tap into a power that overcomes our inability to help others. That power is God's love.

Paul's Greek could be translated this way: "faith is energized through love." God's love, seen in the cross of Jesus, energizes us to work for others—so that we keep going and going. Christian freedom means being free from the things that hold us back so that we can serve.

Since we have been justified—made right with God—we are freed from worrying about ourselves. We want to do good deeds because we are made right with God, not in order to make ourselves right with God. God frees us to turn our energies to others.

Discuss the following items in groups of three. Try to talk with people with whom you have not visited recently.

- Give examples of people you know who allow their faith to work through love.

- What do you think motivates them to live this way?

- Are there any differences between them and you?

- What in Christianity energizes you to keep "going and going"?

■ In what area of your life would you like the power of God's love to step in and energize your faith more fully?

> a. Family life.
> b. Workplace.
> c. Relationships within your church.
> d. Your relationship to the church.
> e. Care for self.
> f. The environment.
> g. Social, political, and economic issues.
> h. Other.

■ What would you like to ask from God in order to more fully energize your faith in this area of your life?

■ Galatians 5:7 talks about running. Think of yourself as a Christian runner. You are running the course of your life. What kind of runner are you?

> a. A sprinter (good for the short distances).
> b. A hurdler (able to overcome obstacles).
> c. A distance runner (able to keep up a steady pace, good for the long haul).
> d. A relay team member (good on my own, but better with others).
> e. A spectator (it's hard to enter in).

■ What kind of "muscle cramps" or other obstacles hinder you from running well your race of life?

A further look

Read James 2:14-18; Hebrews 12:1-2; and 1 Corinthians 9:24-25.

■ What "works" is God calling you to do?

■ What does it mean for you to run your "race of life" with patience and endurance?

Discovery

Galatians 5:13-14

13 For you were called to freedom, brothers and sisters; only do not use your freedom as an opportunity for self-indulgence, but through love become slaves to one another. 14 For the whole law is summed up in a single commandment, "You shall love your neighbor as yourself."

Love your neighbor as yourself

God, Paul reminded his readers, has called us to freedom. But freedom can be misused. We can view it as the opening to do whatever we want, free of responsibility to others. So the very gift of freedom can become an excuse for self-indulgence.

The word translated as "self-indulgence" is actually the word *flesh*. Flesh, for Paul, did not refer simply to our bodies. Rather, the term designated persons as they misused the body by placing themselves at the center of existence. Flesh is a shorthand way to talk about self-centeredness. That is not what Christian freedom is designed to be, since the cross of Jesus is absolutely opposed to a self-serving existence. Jesus "came not to be served but to serve" (Mark 10:45).

Paul's answer to the problem is in Galatians 5:13b—be slaves. How? Through love. Christians are free and captive—free from ourselves and free from trying to save ourselves, but we are also captive as slaves to God and others (Romans 6:15-23). But we are slaves because the love of God has worked in us to turn us from ourselves to serve other people.

And so Paul could say that the entire Mosaic law is summarized in one commandment—love your neighbor as yourself. In loving the neighbor, we turn from placing ourselves at the center to discover and serve the needs of others, even as God in Christ has served us.

Discuss as a group.

■ Martin Luther wrote: "A Christian is a perfectly free lord of all, subject to none. A Christian is a perfectly dutiful servant of all, subject to all." (From *Luther's Works* Vol. 31, copyright © 1957 Muhlenberg Press.) What does this mean to you?

■ A few months after he became president of South Africa, Nelson Mandela visited Poolsmoor Prison. He had been a prisoner there from 1982 to 1988. In what ways was Mandela free when he was a prisoner? In what ways was he a captive (for example, to the needs of his people) once he was free?

■ Marcus Borg wrote that Christ moves us to a "freedom to spend and to be spent in a more overarching, compassionate mission in life." List two ways in which God may be calling you to "be spent." Focus on your life right now.

Respond as a group.

Consider this

A pastor complained that people who came from fundamentalistic churches often felt a tremendous sense of relief when they heard the gospel of God's free gift of love. But after a while, he discovered, they took their faith for granted. Since no one was ordering them to do good in order to be saved, they didn't see any need to be engaged in good deeds or to love others.

Frederick Buechner wrote, "By loving God and your neighbors, Jesus doesn't mean loving as primarily a feeling. Instead he seems to mean that whether or not any feeling is involved, loving God means honoring and obeying and staying in constant touch with God, and loving your neighbors means acting in their best interests no matter what, even if personally you can't stand them."

From *Whistling in the Dark* by Frederick Buechner (San Francisco: HarperSanFrancisco, 1988).

■ In what ways is the "law of love" (Galatians 5:14) open-ended? How does it place a demand on us?

■ How can we love someone we can't stand?

A further look

Read 1 Peter 2:13-17; 1 Corinthians 8:9; and Romans 13:8-10.

■ What does it mean in your life tomorrow to "honor everyone"?

■ How can your Christian liberty be misused and thus harm other people?

■ In light of our study, how would you define love?

Discovery

Galatians 5:16-17b, 19-21a, 22-23a, 26

16 Live by the Spirit, I say, and do not gratify the desires of the flesh. 17 For what the flesh desires is opposed to the Spirit, and what the Spirit desires is opposed to the flesh; . . . 19 Now the works of the flesh are obvious: fornication, impurity, licentiousness, 20 idolatry, sorcery, enmities, strife, jealousy, anger, quarrels, dissensions, factions, 21 envy, drunkenness, carousing, and things like these. . . . 22 By contrast, the fruit of the Spirit is love, joy, peace, patience, kindness, generosity, faithfulness, 23 gentleness, and self-control. . . . 26 Let us not become conceited, competing against one another, envying one another.

The Spirit: A new center for our lives

The flesh—misguided human existence—is powerful. The power that stands over against the flesh, for Paul, is the Spirit. And the Spirit provides a new center for our lives as well as a new power. Around that center and through that power we can reconstruct our daily living.

Since the Spirit is the principle of our new life in Christ, it stands in sharp opposition to the flesh. For that reason Paul set up two lists—the works of the flesh and the fruit of the Spirit.

The works of the flesh (the self-centered "I") are listed first. While some of them are certainly physical, many of the works of the flesh deal with mind or attitude. Idolatry, strife, jealousy, anger, quarrels, envy, and other terms deal with our relationships with other people.

On the opposite side of Paul's spectrum stand the fruits of the Spirit. The first is love. That fruit is the basic product; in a sense the other fruits listed are applications of love in human relationships. Each term also represents a certain forgetting of the self, as the Spirit works in us to turn us outward to others. Love, in all its many manifestations, is the mark of the Spirit.

The final verse is a reminder to Christians to live together in mutual support and concern. It is easy to tear down but much harder to build up each other (see 1 Corinthians 8:1; 10:23).

■ On the following continuum, mark the spot that best indicates the power that dominates your life.

1	2	3	4	5	6	7	8	9	10
Flesh									**Holy Spirit**

■ Is your life to this point where you want it to be? What examples of "flesh" stand in your way?

■ List three ways in which the Holy Spirit is the center of your life or directs your life.

■ Our society does not encourage moral living. What sort of help do you as a Christian need in order to lead a life guided by the Spirit?

■ Which two fruits of the Spirit (5:22-23a) do you most need to cultivate in your interpersonal relationships during the next two weeks? What steps will you take to use the fruit?

Consider this

Marcus Borg, a professor at Oregon State University, said in an interview: "We live our lives much of the time in a self-preoccupied way, in a burdened way that feels cut off from the vital center of energy. And so the central spiritual-psychological issue in the Christian life is the need for internal transformation from a selfish way of being to a way that is free from that."

From "Beyond Belief" in *The Lutheran* (July 1994), copyright © 1994 Augsburg Fortress.

■ **Do you agree? Explain.**

A further look

Read James 1:22-25; 1 Corinthians 9:19; and Philippians 1:9-11.

■ Which do you think is more important for Christians: doing or believing?

■ In what ways can serving others be a witness to them?

Wrap-up

Before you go, take time for the following:

- Group ministry task

- Review

- Personal concerns and prayer concerns

- Closing prayers

Daily walk

Bible readings

Day 1
James 3:13-18

Day 2
Ephesians 5:6-11

Day 3
2 Corinthians 6:3-10

Day 4
1 Timothy 4:12

Day 5
1 Timothy 6:11-15

Day 6
2 Timothy 2:22-26

Day 7
2 Peter 1:5-8

Thought for the journey

Christ frees us. In that freedom we are so liberated from trying to save ourselves that we can serve others.

Prayer for the journey

Free us, our loving God, from ourselves, from our need to place ourselves at the center. Free us to serve others and through them to serve you. Amen.

Verse for the journey

"Do not use your freedom as an opportunity for self-indulgence, but through love become slaves to one another" (Galatians 5:13b).

6 Christian Freedom: Growth in Service

Focus

Because of God's gifts to us, we are freed for others. Growth in service results in a renewed and profound sense of freedom for Christian living.

Community building

You have shared much with each other and have learned much from each other.

- For every person in the group other than yourself, write on a separate card your response to the following statements:

  a. What [name of person] taught me during this course.
  b. How [name] has challenged me.
  c. Two things I want to thank [name] for.

- Give each person the cards written for her or him. After giving people a few moments to read their cards, have a time to share an impression, a surprise, or something otherwise gained by reading or writing the cards.

- Pray for each other by name.

Option

How has the group's ministry task gone? Discuss the task, including these questions: What has gone well? What hasn't gone so well? How has the ministry task affected your group? How has the task affected individuals in the group?

Complete this sentence: "I think the ministry task has been . . ."

Opening prayer

You have given us so much, O Lord. This day we thank you for the gift of the Christian church. Keep us free so that we can serve you in and through it. In the name of Jesus we pray. Amen.

Discovery

Galatians 6:1-2

1 My friends, if anyone is detected in a transgression, you who have received the Spirit should restore such a one in a spirit of gentleness. Take care that you yourselves are not tempted. 2Bear one another's burdens, and in this way you will fulfill the law of Christ.

Freedom for service to others

Galatians 3–4 talked about freedom *from*. Galatians 5–6 deals with freedom *for*, specifically freedom for service to others. In chapter 5 Paul spoke of living and being guided by the Spirit. In chapter 6 he wrote about what that means for life in the Christian community.

The first topic addressed by Paul was that of restoring a sinner to the community. He directed it to "you who have received the Spirit." That phrase may refer to a small group that claimed this title or it may refer to all members of the church, since all have received the Spirit (3:2). In either case, those who have not transgressed are directed not to congratulate themselves on their good morality but rather to reach out to the transgressor.

This is a family matter. Paul wrote to "my friends," or more literally, "my brothers/sisters." Within this family the restoration is to happen "in a spirit of gentleness" (see 5:23). Paul was less concerned with the transgression and more concerned here with the attitude of the one who had not transgressed. Perhaps he had in mind the fact that all of us will sin; no one is perfect. And so as we seek to restore another to the community, we know that we ourselves will be tempted. And that helps us to approach the other person without being arrogant or condescending. We, too, have been or will be in a similar position.

In 6:2 Paul broadened his concern. "Bear one another's burdens." Instead of being ready to condemn and criticize each other, Paul said, be ready to help others shoulder their burdens. In that way a person fulfills Christ's law, which takes us back to 5:14: "'You shall love your neighbor as yourself.'"

Discuss as a group.

■ Galatians 6:1 is directed at members of the Christian family. With what person do you need to seek reconciliation this week? Think of a member of your nuclear or extended family or of your church family who needs to be restored. Without necessarily revealing the person or the details of the situation, share a gentle step you can take to bring reconciliation or restoration.

Respond in pairs.

■ Think of a time when someone has confronted you with an error or sin and has restored you to the relationship "in a spirit of gentleness." Share appropriate details with one other person. How did the process of restoration feel to you?

■ Discuss with another person the three major burdens you are carrying right now. Who is helping you carry those burdens? Whose burdens, other than your own, are you helping to bear?

Discuss as a group.

■ Paul was concerned about our response to others when they are in need of restoration. He wrote, "Take care that you yourselves are not tempted" (6:1b). What can get in the way of a more caring and gentle response to others?

Choose one and explain.

    a. A frustration with an unrelated situation that gets vented by our attacks on another person.
    b. A frustration with an unrelated, hurtful relationship that gets vented by an attack on another person.
    c. Our own low self-esteem at the time of another person's transgression.
    d. Our lack of humility.
    e. An unrepentant spirit.
    f. Our own works of the flesh (Galatians 5:19-21).
    g. Not taking time to pray for the other person in need of restoration.
    h. Other.

■ How does the church help people carry their burdens? How might it do better?

A further look

Read Matthew 18:15-20; Romans 15:1-3; and John 13:34-35.

■ Think of the last time you spoke ill of someone or spread gossip. How does your action fit or not fit with Matthew 18? Pray about that experience.

■ How can Jesus command love? What does that command mean for your life tomorrow morning?

Galatians 6:8-10

⁸ **If you sow to your own flesh, you will reap corruption from the flesh; but if you sow to the Spirit, you will reap eternal life from the Spirit. ⁹So let us not grow weary in doing what is right, for we will reap at harvest-time, if we do not give up. ¹⁰So then, whenever we have an opportunity, let us work for the good of all, and especially for those of the family of faith.**

How should we live in freedom?

In the recent past, the Palestinians have begun to regain a homeland, and blacks in South Africa have gained political freedom. The first question after freedom comes is: How are we to live now that we are free? In verse 8 Paul continued to answer that question for Christians.

Using the pattern he developed in 5:16-25, Paul wrote of flesh and Spirit. All people sow seed—in a sense, the seed of their lives. That life-seed can be sown so that it serves only the individual person in a selfish way. The opposite way of "farming" is to sow one's life-seed to the Spirit. That is, lay hold of Christ in faith in every situation. From that sowing comes eternal life. And from that sowing comes freedom, for "where the Spirit of the Lord is, there is freedom" (2 Corinthians 3:17).

This sowing frees us to live new lives in the present, doing not our own thing but God's own thing as we serve others. Growth in service results in a renewed and profound sense of the freedom God gives us for Christian living. And so we do "not grow weary in doing what is right."

In 6:10 Paul invited the Galatians to "work for the good of all, and especially for those of the family of faith." He turned his readers in two directions. First, to other members of the church. Christians have a special bond with each other and need to be attentive to each other. We owe each other mutual support. But that bond is not meant to keep other people away. And so Christians are, secondly, to "work for the good of all." For that reason, Christians throughout the centuries have served the physical, emotional, and spiritual needs of all people—members of the church or not.

■ Think of a time when you lost yourself in helping some-one else—a youth group service project, delivering Meals on Wheels, working on a Habitat for Humanity house, or aiding an ill neighbor. How did it make you feel?

■ What are you symbolically planting in your life? Think of two plants. Name them, describe why you chose them, and list what fruit you think they will bear. Examples:

Plant	*Why chosen*	*Fruit*
Strawberry	Takes several years to cultivate a good crop	Long-term service to others
Bitter herbs	Ongoing arguments with child or parent	Anger, frustration

■ When do you "grow weary in doing what is right"? How can you renew your energy?

■ Read Galatians 6:1-10 and list the many aspects Paul mentioned about how Christians are to live with each other. How do you experience or not experience these aspects in your own Christian life?

Consider this

Bob had grown up in a home where alcohol was king. Verbal and physical abuse came daily. All Bob could talk about was his goal—freedom from his parents and their drinking. He held on until graduation and went to a college three states away. At Thanksgiving he visited us. He was free, and it was exhilarating. But he was still unsure, for while he was free from his parents, he lacked direction. He graduated from college, entered the Peace Corps, and did physical therapy with orphaned boys in Southeast Asia. The letters he wrote took on a new tone. His work with the boys had given him new purpose, direction, and meaning. He was no longer only free from his parents. He was now free to serve others. Bob had learned that the gift of freedom from God is most fully experienced as service. Once Bob was taken out of himself, in a real sense he came home.

■ Share other stories where you or someone else you know was set free by being captive to the needs of others or of creation in general.

A further look

Read Romans 7:1-6; Ephesians 5:15-20; and 2 Corinthians 4:1-2,16-18.

- Who owns you? How does that ownership determine the fruit you bear?

- What is your ultimate goal in life? How does that goal keep you from losing heart?

Discovery

Galatians 6:14-16

14 May I never boast of anything except the cross of our Lord Jesus Christ, by which the world has been crucified to me, and I to the world. 15For neither circumcision nor uncircumcision is anything; but a new creation is everything! 16As for those who will follow this rule—peace be upon them, and mercy, and upon the Israel of God.

Boasting in the cross of Jesus

Boasting often finds a home in our religious life. In 6:13 Paul wrote about people who boasted in the flesh, a boasting he also had done (Philippians 3:4-6), as he pointed to all the labels that made him important. Others could boast in God's law (Romans 2:23) and their claim to be able to fulfill it. For Paul such boasting is excluded from the Christian life (Romans 3:27). The only kind of boasting proper for Christians is the cross of Jesus, a cross that immediately calls into question any attempt of ours to glory in our accomplishments or status.

Through that same cross, the world's normal values are turned upside down. And so "the world has been crucified to me, and I to the world." That double crucifixion results, once more, in freedom. It is freedom from being judged by the world's standards. Once we are freed from worrying about what others think of us, we are freed to serve, freed to be captive to the will of God. We are free to get our hands dirty in God's service.

In 6:15 Paul restated earlier themes from the letter as he moved toward ending his correspondence. The old standards of circumcision and uncircumcision no longer count. What does count is the new thing God is doing—God is recreating the world and us (2 Corinthians 5:17).

Peace and mercy are the result of this new creation and of the new kind of living to which Paul calls us. These gifts are given to the "Israel of God," meaning all people, whether Jew or non-Jew, who trust in Paul's message of freedom.

Discuss as a group.

Check any that apply.

■ How do you feel about boasting?

___ Boasting is always wrong.
___ A little boasting is okay, but it is dangerous.
___ It's all right to boast about others but not about myself.
___ It's positive to think good things about myself, but it isn't helpful to mention them to others.
___ It's good to boast about what God has done.
___ Other.

■ How free are you of societal standards? In what ways are you not free?

Explore and relate.

■ Where in your life and relationships are you experiencing peace? Where not? Where in your life could you use a little more mercy? Where could you offer more mercy in your relationships? Pray together about these issues.

Discuss these questions as a whole group.

■ This is the last session of this study. What new understandings have you gained? What new attitudes do you have? How will you live differently tomorrow because of studying *Captive and Free* with your small group?

A further look

Read 1 Corinthians 1:26-31; Philippians 2:5-11; and Philippians 4:4-7.

■ How can we boast in the presence of God?

■ Jesus came as a slave to serve. What is God telling us through the life of Jesus?

Wrap-up

Before you go, take time for the following:

- ■ Group ministry task

- ■ Review

- ■ Personal concerns and prayer concerns

- ■ Closing prayers

Daily walk

Bible readings

Day 1
Mark 10:41-45

Day 2
Luke 22:24-27

Day 3
John 12:20-26

Day 4
1 Peter 4:7-11

Day 5
1 Corinthians 12:4-11

Day 6
Romans 12:3-8

Day 7
Romans 12:9-21

Thought for the journey

"You give yourself to us, O Lord; / Then selfless let us be, / To serve each other in your name / In truth and charity."

Prayer for the journey

Our gracious God, you have given us so much. Continue to move us to serve others as you have served us. We pray in the name of Jesus. Amen.

Verse for the journey

"Let us work for the good of all, and especially for those of the family of faith" (Galatians 6:10).

Appendix

Group directory

Record information about group members here.

Names	Addresses	Phone Numbers

Group commitments

"Do not be conformed to this world, but be transformed by the renewing of your minds, so that you may discern what is the will of God—what is good and acceptable and perfect" (Romans 12:2).

■ For our time together, we have made the following commitments to each other

■ Goals for our study of this topic are

■ Our group ministry task is

■ My personal action plan is

Prayer requests

Prayers

■ Closing Prayer

Lord God, you have called your servants to ventures of which we cannot see the ending, by paths as yet untrodden, through perils unknown. Give us faith to go out with good courage, not knowing where we go, but only that your hand is leading us and your love supporting us; through Jesus Christ our Lord. Amen.

Lutheran Book of Worship, copyright © 1978, 153.

(If you plan to use the Lord's Prayer, record the version your group uses in the next column.)

■ The Lord's Prayer

Resources

Cousar, Charles. *Galatians.* Interpretation. Atlanta: John Knox, 1982.

Krentz, Edgar. *Galatians.* Augsburg Commentary on the New Testament. Minneapolis: Augsburg, 1985.

Lahrmann, Dieter. *Galatians: A Continental Commentary.* Trans. O. C. Dean, Jr. Minneapolis: Fortress, 1992.

Luther, Martin. *Lectures on Galatians.* Volumes XXVI and XXVII of *Luther's Works,* trans. and ed. Jaroslav Pelikan. St. Louis: Concordia, 1963-64.

Matera, Frank J. *Galatians.* Sacra Pagina. Collegeville, Minn.: The Liturgical Press, 1992.

Soards, Marion L. *The Apostle Paul: An Introduction to His Writings and Teaching.* Mahwah, N.J.: Paulist, 1987.

Taylor, Walter F., Jr. "Session 13: The Letters of Paul." *Mission90: Bible Study and Witness.* Minneapolis: Augsburg Fortress, 1991.

Please tell us about your experience with INTERSECTIONS.

4. What I like best about my INTERSECTIONS experience is

5. Three things I want to see the same in future INTERSECTIONS books are

6. Three things I might change in future INTERSECTIONS books are

7. Topics I would like developed for new INTERSECTIONS books are

8. Our group had _____ sessions for the six chapters of this book

9. Other comments I have about INTERSECTIONS are

_____

Thank you for taking the time to fill out and return this questionnaire.

---------------------------------FOLD CARD IN HERE, SEAL WITH TAPE, AND MAIL TODAY!---------------------------------

Please check the INTERSECTIONS book you are evaluating.

☐ Following Jesus   ☐ Death and Grief   ☐ Men and Women

☐ The Bible and Life   ☐ Divorce   ☐ Peace

☐ Captive and Free   ☐ Faith   ☐ Praying

☐ Caring and Community   ☐ Jesus: Divine and Human   ☐ Self-Esteem

Please tell us about your small group.

1. Our group had an average attendance of _____.

2. Our group was made up of
   _____ Young adults (19-25 years)
   _____ Adults (most between 25-45 years)
   _____ Adults (most between 45-60 years)
   _____ Adults (most between 60-75 years)
   _____ Adults (most 75 and over)
   _____ Adults (wide mix of ages)
   _____ Men (number) and _____ women (number)

3. Our group (answer as many as apply)
   _____ came together for the sole purpose of studying this INTERSECTIONS book.
   _____ has decided to study another INTERSECTIONS book.
   _____ is an ongoing Sunday school group.
   _____ met at a time other than Sunday morning.
   _____ had only one facilitator for this study.

BUSINESS REPLY MAIL

FIRST-CLASS MAIL   PERMIT NO. 22120   MINNEAPOLIS, MN

POSTAGE WILL BE PAID BY ADDRESSEE

Augsburg Fortress

ATTN INTERSECTIONS TEAM
PO BOX 1209
MINNEAPOLIS MN 55440-8807